Phenomena

What we must say can be discovered,
whispered, in the overbreath
of what lies on a piece of paper,
there is a music produced out somewhere,
outside and over what is put down in words.
Words can only carry us, on away,
to what waits so splendidly
and purely and overwhelmingly unspeakable,
we are delivered to that.
—William Goyen

Phenomena

Poems by Cathryn Hankla

University of Missouri Press
Columbia & London
1983

A Breakthrough Book
Number 40

Copyright © 1983 by Cathryn Hankla
University of Missouri Press, Columbia, Missouri 65211
Printed and bound in the United States of America
All rights reserved
Library of Congress Catalog Card Number 82–11013

Library of Congress Cataloging in Publication Data

Hankla, Cathryn, 1958–
    Phenomena : poems.

    (A Breakthrough book ; no. 40)
    I. Title. II. Series.
PS3558.A4689P5 1983   811'.54   82–11013
ISBN 0–8262–0386–8

Grateful acknowledgment is made to the following magazines for publishing these poems and for allowing them to be reprinted: "I Dream My Return," "Swift Current," "The First Prayer of Angles," "Sleeping in the Loft of Dreams," *Artemis*; "The Promised Coat," first published in *Intro 10*, copyright Associated Writing Programs; "The Dispute Over Bodies in Water," first published in *Intro 11*, copyright Associated Writing Programs; "Volume 13: Jirasek to Lighthouses," first published in *Intro 13*, copyright Associated Writing Programs; "Answering the Past," "A Moment of Violence," "Firefly," *Outerbridge*; "Nothing Is Obvious," *New Virginia Review Inc.*; "Earth & Apples," *Mid-American Review*; "The Fate of Waking," *Alchemy*; "Walking in the Path of the Moon," "The Night-Father Was Found Alive," *Mississippi Valley Review*; "A White Horse," *The New Jersey Poetry Journal*; "Mockingbird," *Quarterly West*.

for Richard

Every good gift and every perfect gift
is from above, and cometh down
from the Father of lights,
with whom is no variableness,
neither shadow of turning.
James 1:17

Contents

A Tunnel to the Moon

1. *The Dark Side*
Through a telescope or a spyglass drawn from a coat
you gaze, blink upon the floating dust spurs
of the dark side of the moon.
A tatter in your sleeve irritates your elbow
every time you move the piece from pocket to eye.
You see a moon shell fall from the back
of a snail. You study its small antennae.
Stars stir like legs just up from sleep.

A woman's head is ready to fly off.
A tire spins on white ice spurting questions.
Wheels spit, you need to snap
them to a stop, but you are tired.
It is the instant of an eye drawn back,
the second you would have kissed off-camera
had the reel not split.
It is like a butterfly spun from a lariat
or specks of silver smoke around your wrist:
fast minutes when you ripped through the last
ten pages to close the finished book wondering.

2. *Edges, Surprises*
Twirl in dark fuchsia and black, your cape.
A tear on your shoulder flaps in the wind,
and it is autumn, it is autumn.

The crack in the mirror lets legs slide
out from under you. You slip
on leaves, you trip over paper figs;
tremble like a new-hatched calf,
your skin is rough and brushed backward.
You could be standing on pins, or
falling off a swinging bridge. A pig's
tail coils, stretches taut as a tightrope.

You have to work to keep on edges.

Will you wear the wind
like a wing, wind in the empty
ring of rope with your hand?

A fist pokes through the window
in the wood making a knob for the door,
opening into an unlined palm
(you must touch with purpose
if you touch at all).

It waves a quick hello and disappears.

3. *20th of March 1970*
It is your twelfth birthday.
You spring from the box like
tiny pink candles balanced
in icing. You sway and drip
with light like you have
just been born, like you have
just been wiped by silk cloth.
You tilt on your patent heels
and spin in a patch of sun.
You have begun to notice
a stirring in the buds of trees,
new yellow-green on the thin
sleeping limbs. You are shining
like a leaf. You dip
and sway with the day like
your first two-wheeled ride
seven birthdays ago.
You are costumed for a Méliès
movie, a chorus girl
waving good-bye to the human bullet,
whisked into the moon's eye
by a cannon blast.
You are bending down, getting sand

under white cotton socks, you are
finding false angel wings.
It is like hearing an airplane
touch down,
or your first sudden
notice of spring.

4. *The Light*
Trust in air,
in warm puffs of steam rising:
you stayed long in someone else's
morning wrapped under quilts
like unopened print.
The time you wrestled in your room
in your own friend's arms, light moved
like darts through branches,
oranges and roses appeared from lost summer
and you thought it was spring in early December.
You are as near to that time as cloth to skin.
Sweaters rub your neck. Soft yarn strokes
your sore throat like smooth, luke liquid
sliding inside your stomach, making you start
and ignite like the first quick touch
from someone you already love.

Paradox of Gravity

The day has begun crossing
continents. Subjects from sleep
coincide, oil on water and the colors
call him up.

He puts on glasses and squints
at the sun. Overhead, there
is a hum of planes, an echo
that bounces between clouds.

He holds a mirror to move
a spot of sun or a magnifying glass
concave to focus:
a fire begins on the limb of a foreign tree
as his flame burns a crisp leaf.
Coincidence. The day circles
like trim green blades beneath a foot,
bends sun through a bowl.

He squints at the sun, becomes
a yellow lemon, the mind of an egg
that wobbles on a sill. He is as fragile
as a unicycle wheel.

The day is an audience of cows
turning around in a row
to scowl. A fence holds them back
across the creek. He blinks
both eyes—he has decided
to turn into a tree.

All afternoon he bruises his shins
on stones and thinks of telephone poles
stretched with wire. Someone has polished
the grass under him. He slides in the wind.
He sees his face alive
on the glossed hoods of cars,
enameled and wide-angled.
Somewhere between the tree and its reflection
he is lost.

The Water Is the Skin of the River

"Mister, is the Thames the water,
or the hole it goes in?"

—Fynn, *Mister God, This Is Anna*

Over the river, the bone
buried like a spine within,
birds swim on air.
While underneath the skin
fish begin to whistle, crawling
quietly among themselves,
for it is their day of prayer.

Into the water a fish prepares to fly
circles. There is a cunning to this
mission that deceives the eye,
birds swim, fish fly. But,
seeing will not tell us. Invisible air,
water thick as color.

Nor will I explain, renaming
wings, calling them fins—
compare each to a fan and then
reduce them to the same. Water holds
no man. Try calling water, *skin*.
Consider it a game. Consider
wrinkles, *waves*; freckles, *rocks*;
currents, veins.

Listen to the pulse with an ear
on the wake, the beat is beneath
the whistles, the whispers of swimmers
seeking familiar places. How light
their bones have become
diving and leaping. The spine
of the river pulls down with gravity.

They dance with fins and wings, with
reverence into other worlds singing.
They know the water is the skin of the river.
Water as a god. Skin as a bridge,
a veil, or netting.
They know no water thin as grace.

Water evaporates, scaling
upward into the invisible. Leaving
the bed of bone shining bright,
reflecting some distant sun.

Possessions

Things belong to people
who want them most.

—Dashiell Hammett

Think, instead, the leather case chose
you. Scarves, those boots, that ring.
Mother-of-pearl, the pinned fish
like a weather vane always pointing
somewhere, an imitation horizon
separating your head into cloud,
your body into mountain.

Most things belong to whom they will.
The day you wore the flowered skirt
as if you wore no skirt. It was
a present clinging to its past
owner. No matter how well matched,
articles always know the way home.

Gifts I buy give themselves away,
bursting before their messenger.
And things that others try to keep
come through the mail addressed to me.
Like dark judgments,
the stubborn shoe which will never fit.

for Dara Wier

The Good-bye-Hello Handbook

A cerulean cat licking the yellow pages
suddenly rubs your bare legs
with embarrassing audacity. You'd do anything
to stop it. The phone is off its hook.
To touch that fluff and not be touched.

Cooking three brown eggs in a wok
with thick, white cheese, you are struck
by the absence of certain objects
and any thoughts of these: no letters, lovers, last
of all, no kitchen buzz of insects.

And the squat, summer horses
laze on the long hill with blond lashes
and matted manes. You have made too much
breakfast, and they watch
enough bland cheese sliced for seven
open-faced sandwiches. You stand alone,
and there is no way to uncut it.

You, a gypsy, packed and bulging with memories,
carry an orange knapsack
filled with quills and bottled ink,
fend the damp rim of a reservoir. You are one
gypsy who constantly dreams of unpacking.
Separation of one thing from another—to spread
paper from pens, books from toilet items,

all your clothes to dry in the expanding sun.
See how moving makes you lean. Quick
to discard and stack boxes, sweeping under carpets
nothing you might forget when you leave again.
You scour white tubs, board floors that splinter,
to lift fingerprints. The tracks
of light living.

But on a certain day, uncertain, as you open
the same door. Like a message
you have missed for some time, it appears on the stoop:
a gift of eucalyptus, rose-colored and real,
its musk lasting long into the inner rooms.
When you return, the bells high within their silo
swing into sound: this is the homeland,

land, a burst of greeting flares the port.
Arms aloft, lithe and waving, hold
your homecoming figure close as their own liquid faces.
You are here, at last, you are here.
If you leave now, there will be bread on every windowsill.

Swift Current

Those promises to mend alone
will not matter
in a room
where passerine birds gather
each current with wings to move
in the hovering stir.
Be careful as you listen,
listing, I will hold your pas seul prayer
to my lips.
Your eyes may start, to see
me curled on the curving surface
of your vision—asleep
in this swift, suspended fall—
air sharpening the trees
until they shatter. Leaves
that break unto our heads like water
draw us to seek together. This face,
in the dark, well may be your own.
Palm opening, you give me a small coin
to close inside my hand. Your words
speak, between the closing distance
of what we desire and dare.
Every soul you are may surface in unison:
all of them walking through this same bare room,
all of them dressed for this weather,
all of them greeting each other, shaking
hands; all of them guests. Cast off at once!
To all the chimneys wave good-bye.
Ashore, each has crossed to bear the same secret.
From the far land no word is witnessed,
but into our lover's ears, dimly we whisper:
What we seek is not ever the answer.
This is the silent narrative
of gifts. You will know grace

by an absence of sunlight. You will know it
when you fear most to know. Its shadow
will follow you, but you will not be harmed.
Everything in the world will be wrong
except your heart.

I Dream My Return

When I come home
my hands are in pockets.
It rains in the yard
as you push your hands after mine
and pull the balled fists from deep inside,
saying nothing. Something in my palms,
I offer you like sugar cubes or seed,
glows with your breath brushing across it.
We plant in random rows,
carrots, potatoes—
what is hidden will nourish us. People
far away know every word we utter,
are with us even now, casting
their shadows on the earth we turn.

The Promised Coat

Already, it is in your eyes
as we look, together, into the rain.
No, you say, as I wrap my coat
around you close as shadow, turning back
the rain-streaked collar, asking you
to, *Please take this.*
You glance at me and go instead,
into the color of water.
No one, alone, finds shelter
here. Through the door frame the rain
has fallen while we've stood
as in a photograph, a long time taken,
and my eyes fall to the wet street
where your footsteps make a sudden stop.
Under lamplight, it is again our eyes
which meet as empty as what they hold.

Answering the Past

My early homecoming catches the dog
steaming in a mist of sheets,
having smuggled his head to sleep
on the pillow, close to the morning
smell of my husband's hair.

Your letter caught me like this.
In dreams, unaware, expectant of nothing,
I opened the first mail sent in hopes
it would be a photograph,
or some object like that
I could keep as a gift.

Instead you sent the shells of eggs,
white crumble of guilt to cut
my palms; grains of salt
from the Great Salt Lake that powdered
my thumbs to take their prints,
so you'd always know where to find me;
pale corner of cloth you snipped
from a favorite shirt;
slip of paper with my name scrawled
bitter as aspirin;
two torn tickets faded by the dark
touch of your hands.

Arrived home to answer this list
of where you've been, I look toward the hidden
mountains I know are there.
This is what I send: the picture
of who I am, dressed in the color of air,
my eyes reflecting an imperfect view.
I promise to forget the past
once again, let the land shift
in the water of my sight, and forgive.

The Dark

The dark lets you walk where you would not walk.
Branches claw your sleeve, thorns push
through the skin of your feet.

You wrap your arms around a mouth, a man's
or a woman's, it is too dim to tell.
Alone in a field, night sounds,

you stoop and palm a rock. It is colorless,
smooth to touch. You toss it up
in any direction, all, you listen.

My Friend Who's Afraid of the Dark

1.
"You should always look into your backseat
before you unlock the door." She tells me
of the new Seville that lights inside
when skin touches the handle.
But my back-bench seat, only as deep
as the width of a tight bathtub,
could not comfortably hide a child.
She has forgotten this.

I, who am startled by objects
illuminated, mornings, in the slanted sun,
see her layered against the darkness
in heavy sleep, her door propped open
with one tennis shoe.

The hall overhead burns. It is dawn.
She sleeps on, her lightless dreams
turning her toward the plaster wall.
I push in the button, switch us
into uneven chiaroscuro, kick
her door closed to make her think,
when she wakes, she has spent
the night completely in the dark.

2.
We stand within the frame, throw back
the door. Whenever the wind slams
it closed, we see a wire screen
webbed through the glass
swing separate from the night.

Raised with heat, our thin gowns balloon.
Between cold air and warm, the blizzard

turns from us into the storm,
never touching unless we force our hands
into its mouth.
The weather sucks at us; we sway
over the fire escape while leaning
against the dark. Behind us

is the hall, extinguished by a power failure.
"I saw this once in a film,"
and pointing at snowflakes, "they swim
like schools of fish." I think of insects,
balance. She says, "Let's fly from here."

3.
"What do you see when you look into the dark?"
She has caught me staring up the stairwell
to the space where the mirror should be.
"Nothing," I return, imagining a broom
on each step, brooms whose stems
strike against the head when traveling
those darker stairs. Something startles her,
and she asks if she may crack my door.

With both doors open, our rooms
connect. There is more light, she thinks,
if we sleep unenclosed. Walls create
corners that absorb our late laughter:
she never says the last word.

for Lisa Kennedy Hicks

Nothing Is Obvious

*Whenever, absentmindedly, I happened to open
my hands, curious objects slid out of them.*

—Murilo Rubiao

We see through the dark circle,
look—nothing there
inside the slick cylinder.

Out comes a linked illusion
of silk scarves. The magician
holds one cupped, puckers
the cloth in his palm.
Pulls the bird from the air.

I know the secret
is the Möbius scarf. But,
you insist on feathers,
each one a clue that sifts
onto the stage. Evidence:

after the show, the magician
sweeps them up himself, tidily
empties the dustpan
into a star-covered box
that fits beneath the cage.

He keeps feathers to construct
another bird. It is obvious, you say.
We travel downtown to the park,
feed peanuts to pigeons. All day
you balance birds on your hands.

White Summer, Museum Piece,
Montague Street in Winter

All day on my hands the scent of orange,
the water of the Thames. White summer,
a Whistler portrait in white, a day in winter
full with black-umbrellaed snow.
On sidewalks the remainder of the night stays
white as shrouds. Underfoot, air-shaken,
you will see it like the past, like the frost
array of white wings printed on stones.
Snapshots take up the street, the distant
sighting, ice-capped, as you write
a postcard, vast and sharp, of something
present; just passing, transparent as absence.

The Touch of Something Solid

We match the southern border
of the north to the north of the south.

By halves, we hang a map
where other things have fallen.

Our hands press the seam,
moving to hold together that state

you say is Texas. In the familiar
places, a kind of tapping

on the surface for all we know:
the touch of topography on the body

of light as line and plummet sounding
in time, the equation unchanging on earth

that binds us again to the word.

for D.

The Dispute over Bodies in Water

> *. . . sinking or not*
> *sinking, rising or not rising. . . .*
> —Galileo

Not bodies of water, seas,
but bodies in water sinking:

slivers of ice, flesh
of any shape as in a dream

you pass from palace to ship,
to grotto or beach and wake

in this room of sleep, a solid body
in its own water afloat.

As if, in dreams, displacement
inclines a departing mass

to find its own
level like water in constant

circuit of the continents
adrift and silent—you have sent

yourself this far on either side,
sent surface falling, risen

to the place from which you started,
a body of water in water.

Earth & Apples

> *. . . what wings raised to the second power*
> *can make things come down without weight?*
>
> —Simone Weil, *Gravity and Grace*

Falling to earth in the orchard
with fruit called magical,
my palms, stinging, cup that touch
of apple left from memories—(secret
shaped upon the hand's breadth
and fitted inside each fist.)

Falling to earth in apples,
my hat lifts off into space.
Tilted over the landscape of grass,
branches stir, leaves
begin twirling
transformed by the invisible.

Whatever shook the ladder sent us
falling, fruit and flesh,
to light on the surface of the earth.
What, in passing, I have shaken
also is ransom for this flight
through air and hurtling of spheres—

The absence of anything is touched
in apples, anything is possible:
that there could be a bouncing
in place of crushed skins, that stem
and core could attempt, within fruit,
a different spin—

that spirit might swing unhurt
when all has fallen or is grass,
that the body, too, might arise,
travel some time alone
and find something, other than
this falling, of its own.

Walking in the Path of the Moon

Water breaks away to pull
its layered shadow. A parachute
buoys like drying shirts. In the distance,
a voice before our lips chants
its lament of broken stucco.
Our likeness walks stretched
as the sun below our shoulders sets
east and west with its crossing near enough
always to compass direction,
to fatten out days like fruit. By signs

our language holds land on water; water
on air; air lifting lighter;
husband, wife. Each to each and linked
by touch. Bare feet, paler than the night,
have born us along the trail
of marked trees, held our bodies where alone
we would not travel. In this lowering of light
we take hands, see the moon divide the dusk,
watching its reflection wash in silver and extend
across whitecaps to us.

Sleeping in the Loft of Dreams

Pale yellow on the new skylight, darkness pulls
the moon inside. The ladder to the loft—
its precarious steps, steep, even in daylight—
a simple two-way passage. Under a clear slant

we trade whatever we can. The rain keeps me
there. He takes down a box and counts
six blue jay feathers into my hand.
I give him the seven white buttons from my blouse.

He cuts his hair with a bowie knife, offers
the bright curl. Now, a box full of buttons
rattles as he closes the lid, until
the rain begins again. Now, my hair

strung with feathers, my palm tight
on the lock. Buckets of rainwater have spilled
over the floor, but the wood in the loft,
split, is dry enough to light.

His dream of two women learning an oriental game
wakes us both. Around his head I wrap my blouse,
cool, to catch fever. The blue feathers fall.
I run remembering the one-winged owl: let go

only to be home, the next day,
sleeping in the loft of dreams.

The Day Without the Dream

Picture the dreamers
on the day without the dream:

weather that stills us—
it is the rain that touches
my felt hat and jewels
the red feather like flame.

You await the call
that will ask you to wait
for my visit. To answer
you must leave it all.

(I am coming and you are not yet free.)

One hand tracing
a keyless chain, I walk alone
in the deep grass of fall
laden with monarch wings.

First on my lips is your name
wondering how you will receive
what it is that I bring. And everything
is sense: the poems, the photographs
exchanged—a balanced dream.

(I am with you and you are not yet free.)

Alone, back turned, you chalk
the blackboard with the words
I have never heard: *I have given
away a ring.* And your heart

directs your hands like a memory
of the dream without the day, the day
without the dream, transparent
day. One without the other

we will all be wed.

The Journey

. . . back to this land where each step
makes the heart beat faster like a step toward love. . . .

—Antoine de Saint Exupéry

Having burned my pink palms
on blue flame; having said,
forever. *Hello*, to the far side;
to the spun coin of the past, *hello*;
to the green Atlantic ocean
drifting wider than the dream.

A month I've known
your name (quick speech).
A month I've felt this rain,
the bold weather of caring,
the quick speech, unfeigned,
reciting one shared answer.

For witness take doors, sunlit
as gold tipped pyramids;
take Jupiter as destiny
ringed and glowing on the winter
horizon; take this memory:

I drew the third eye in fog,
one finger on glass to cry,
Don't leave, don't leave.
When the eye of Egypt opened, I saw
the sign reflected back to me
as you stood before it saying,

Nothing is forgotten, you will see,
it will all return to you
like forgotten fears, like history,
like the solid scripture
you never thought you'd learn.

The First Prayer of Angles

It was only the wing of the plane
that moved as I moved within that body.

It was the moon alone
upside down, I turned my head, pressed my face
to tinted sky too, to see the moon.
Something round, to move around. To have moved
there then back again like this, I have
to focus up through glass.

It was the ocean
for so long it was the same as snow blindness:
too much the same, too little
light, too much, it is much the same.

It was a month of space
too narrow to walk, too wide to cross.
Streets and sidewalks, subway, bus. I must
have found my way the wrong way home time
and time again. And time; how time is not
its own at all, at all. And all the time
I thought what we did made no difference,
what I did was done alone. Secretly,
there are no minutes. In truth, no time.

It has been the blankness of clouds
by night. Flying by night
or the angle of vision stopped down, my face
squinted there, still against the same window.
Remember. I am still there. Now,
as I look to the face of the whitest light
I have ever seen, up to identify
the same features of the moon, my angle
turns down and the channel opens between two
bodies of land. Land, lights spaced
in formation, an island for which I have no name.

It must have been the event of land,
the memory of a much-remembered land,
a land of trees. And though it was midnight,
my time, the memory past
time was clear. We flew
over Manhattan and down the coast, home.

I sight the trees through glass.
Low angle, I see their frailest leaves as limbs
which have gone without light, never again.
And I know. I know the prayer of angels
held, spellbound, on our tongues
like sleep. The prayer itself of air,
another name for felled sheep in sleepy counting.
In time, we will talk together of trees
holding our silence before their wisdom
like the fools we have always been.

Unuttered prayer, unuttered prayer.
What words are there for this single prayer;
this disturbance of shingles flapping
on the roof, ringing in the air, in the bluest
salt breeze: *It must have been the wind*, I say.
And the answer shapes your mouth in the name for *wings*.

Last Night a Light

Last night a light lay down
beside my head; the pillow flowed
beneath the luminous yellow globe.
It told me to be still, *Lay down
your head, your burden of weight,*
and said, *Let a light rain begin.*

Risen at the window to listen,
pressing my hands close, both flat
on the cool glass palms sting;
I am awake. Sing again stung panes,
their clear imprints. Flesh has opened
transparent the dream. Sing simple
rain; singing darkness; sing.

I see the crystal rain fall
through a lamp-lit sphere of sky
and when, instantaneously, I feel
this is not enough—light
chills my skin inside and without
warning with white heat,
like air, meaning sure life; sign;
sear; breath's involuntary message—
there is the sudden gasp of spirited air.

The Night Hunting

A dead deer splits
the dry leaves, hooves to humus,
its smooth flank in the dusk, flesh
toned and white, covered
with flies. Eye upturned and eaten,
bone socket bare: it was the liquid eye,
first, that darkness touched.

Rain struck, I watch the carcass
shedding bullets like blood
until my hands are water
soaked inside both pockets
and the hollow eye socket, flooded, opens
with blue light, it too,
pooling through pale branches.

A Moment of Violence

Is there some wilderness in us
that the wild senses and cannot trust?

It has been a day since the blood
of the jay washed my hands.
Once cleansed with water, now they hold
signs in the heart lines
of their palms. A red river traces
the length of one life.
The broken wing lay cupped, where
a head line is a dark blotch.
And fingernails that touched
the torn beak bear sickle stains.

An imprint remains of this, for after
the moon has grown different and spent,
and the spot in the road
where the rabbit was hit seems to have changed
under light and sunk into blacktop,
blue jays appear apart from other birds.
I look to them with deference
and wish the one I held had lived
or had not shrunk so much away
that to save it would as well have been its death.

I think of the way in which the bird
was buried in a box I had marked for moving,
Care: Enclosed, One Dragon China Bowl
and remember the wasps I killed early summer
in their nest, my surprise
when a sticky mucus adhered to flagstone, red
under my step. I had no awareness
that theirs would be a messy death, that I might feel
regret in having thus protected myself from stings
I'd perhaps have never felt.

A White Horse

        choking in a wind
canters the circle of a hill—
on the crest of a hill, in the center
of a circle—two stone coffins
decorate.

        One keeps an angel
under its lid in place of anything
dead. Death chisels the other, beneath
a cast angelic face.

The round the horse makes
is shucked and the horse's breath
is shortened in its gait,
its mane drawn back, teeth yellow.
Foam dirties its back in a wide scar.

The horse is not the color
of cloud, it is not a ghost charged.
A white horse is winding
to its drum, faster, thin, touched
by flame that clings. It is wound
internally and spun;
being a truth it does not sing.

So Lightly She Must Be Air

A sliver of something under her finger.
She is humming.
Bit of mica—that shining splinter. Her memory
is rivulose, going round with lists,
a roulette of the ancient.
All her friendships are there on the list,
the dead and the living, her sick husband.
—All her generations continue,
and she must keep check.

She has lost something in her dream.
Down corridors she searches the rooms
for the black purse, her handbag full of change,
too heavy to lift.
When she finds it, the green bills
will be spilling from its lip.

She remembers something, the color red:
Christmas, she bids her bridge game in boxes
tied bright with strings. She sings
her murmurs of one suit, *hearts*, alone.
In the hospital hall, a handmade dove twirls
on curled ribbon. She can almost see it
from her chair. High up it luffs
in a standstill spiral. She points and says
what I cannot hear. Her hand is light on me,
its bones like hollow sparrows,
while I call into the air:

stuffed, *white*, *bird*, and finally, *dove—peace*
that crosses my lips
like a whisper she has had to bear, forgotten
to ask what it was.

for Bonnie

Mockingbird

I hear your knock in the chimney,
in the soot where you are locked
by glass. Your flutter trills,
its echo answers from the bush
full of thorns, dark wilted berries,
empty nests. Three frail
yellow beaks blather silent
for their feed. And their mother
is here, perched on the iron grate,
chirping so seldom she will stay
nearly all the daylight hours
before I find her, closed eyes
against thirst. I shut off the house
and open the glass, the kitchen door.
Will she fly out, will she fly? No,
she's shut her black eyes and huddled
next to the blackened heat-brick back
of the absent fire, too tired to budge.
I take a checked dish towel,
flag her across to open air.
I hold my breath, for she is flapping
her head into ceiling,
into molding, but then the open way
her wings are striped, white and black,
the way she doesn't turn back—I breathe
out, look up to dust away the down
spotting paint above my reach.
Straight to her nest, she beats the dusk.

The Fate of Waking

1.
In the dream you pointed to the place
in time your father would float
facing the silt like a trapped relic
of a saint. When you held his purple skin
against your own, his became a luminous body,
the weight of a child in your arms.

Seated on a doorsill
near the southern tip of Spain,
you are looking out to sea
where sails unfurl ice blue and lazy,
where water caps an infinitude of white.
Back home there are sweet rolls,
chocolates in the hollow shapes
you've never liked.
But still it is home, not Italy
or Paris where you've lived, or here:
the tip of Spain, a port,
this doorsill where you think of a land
far from any place.

The land rises in your memory
along the stiffness in your shoulders
putting into mind the words of a woman
whose hands felt as mine do,
as cool on your forehead,
now as light on your neck.
You rock in her arms
under limbs of maple,
the red leaves of October

and circle a bird in the sky.
Your vision squints
the way a child holds finger and thumb
to measure, in the distance, a house or tree
chanting the names of objects seen.
Sails babble in the wind, you stand
to listen; your hands are shy,
washed soft by water, they shift untouched
in pockets balanced palm to palm.

Your mother's voice calls across green grass,
forsythia, a field of spotted cows.
And you answer with the slow feathering
breeze as it lifts down
on the belly of a bird, darkness
cupped in both your hands.

On water you see the dream, your memory
of what is past.
You have seen yourself
in the dream, dreamer and dreamed,
remembered yourself in the present,
and now you see
your father floating face down.
You know there is nothing to erase this vision.

If, in sleep, you speak of the water,
my voice covers yours with its shadow.
You are the dreamer
in the space of time at sea level.
I'll edge you into waking to give up dreams
like ghosts, take your tongue, and for an instant,
hold it on my own
to teach it the first speech of separation.

2.

My hands pressed blood to his brain,
covered the wound
but would not stop the skull's
radical whittling of bone,
its dismiss of the human.

I had imagined the dream
killing like a cancer,
in the end closing
my throat with its clot
to take back the gift of voice.

It is years since I saw him asleep
in the sea, years since
the story of a dream death
that could kill as easily
as the power of memory.

When my father died from the gun-
shot wound, I was able to rise
from the vision. What I want back
is bone before it became white symbol;
the last grace of remembering.

3.
On winter air, the church
is burning. I touch windows steamed
with breath, see darkness broken up
by flames, dry smoke ascend
like searchlights beam into the sky.

Phosphorescent fire trucks,
the congregation arrived with buckets,
do nothing but witness the gutting
of the sanctuary—save only the altar
cross, hardwood that will not split.

Like ghosts the people sing, "Let Us Wash
In The Blood Of The Lamb," the baptismal hymn
when I filled my lungs beneath water
sprinkled off the preacher's palm.
Each word on their tongues like stigmata.

A hole like the charred mark
where a meteorite has fallen lifting dirt.
Hands of Jesus, his feet scarred—
here is the heart of the earth,
the stopping place of everything on earth.

4.
Rain drummed the dead
girl the sheriff found
stuffed with kerosene soaked
cloth that had ignited
but failed to burn her body up.

Three days before, during
the door-to-door church census,
the rapist slit her down
from the navel
and gutted her like squirrel.

Across state lines, the killer
is behind bars for another crime.
I coil the newspaper, raise it
to pan a passing car.
The space between the driver

and the passenger is small.
Driving, the blade separates
her ribs, reaches as far
as his arm can go. He keeps
his eyes on the dotted road.

5.

Like Symmes I will go
to the center of the globe,
bore at both poles
to find the hollow space,
to see myself on the surface

of the hollow sea.
At the center of that water
I will search for the mouth
of the single trout
once pulled out by its tail.

Of transparent meat
turned white with heat,
the solid part will be the heart.
To eat, I'll sink my teeth
until they touch

and think the fish
is balanced like the taste
of salt over my tongue.
I wish to drink
this elemental spirit,

food wedded to me
as the changeling of energy.
Water of fire,
and the heart of matter,
fish that is the bone of light.

6.

An empty eye is the glutton of sight.
It sees its own concentric
darkness fuse with objects
to make any day a dawn of death.
It is the sin of self-punishment.

Before I guessed the depths of atoms
the universe stretched to cover me,
infinite. I found Arcturus
by looking up, Pluto and later, electrons
with a scope and its reverse.

Inside these spheres, when I
have learned there is always
something else to see, in any direction
the field of what is visible opens
to illuminate more mystery.

My hollow skull, my hollow eye,
my cells filled with what is weightless.
The long event of life
as echo answering some shout
that happened to land in the way of surfaces.

7.
A memory of snow
like the memory of your birth
in a mist. You decide you must
enter the midst of the earth
in alligator skin.
When the white hits its roughness
you are lost, white
as the day in your first

dream of snow:
Christmas in the London streets
strung with colored lights
like the leaves in the fall of your birth.
Music, the memory
of your future. You must play
clarinet in a marching band.
But today the street players
blow flurries from their horns
like whales in a fury of tuning chords.
Clouds turn as you leap, arms raised,
seventy stories to the roof—gaze
down through a tunnel of structures
to the constellations, stars
of color and snow
far in the street, below.
Free-falling, you see yourself
somersaulting, air-swimming, -skidding,
-spinning in antigravity,
flat-footed to land. Event

of memory like the dream:
your memory of your dream
of birth. The snow
enters today becoming memory,
an event
in the mist of days.

8.
Krakatoa is west of Java

What water shifts
forms into island.
Composed of lava flows,
it is not volcano or cone-shaped
mountain. It is not the four-mile crater.

It is not the filaments of as many lamps
to light a sky ash-shaken
or red sunsets
as fine dust drifts
through a year of stratosphere.

Not cloud of cinder
or ether of ash or any idea of permanence.
Krakatoa, East of Java:
a film of hollow triumph,
the triumph of utter transience.

In difficult darkness
a screen falls vertical to form, before
the eye, what water shifts away from.
An island of light, the mountain of light—
the eye's mythic history of life.

Motions of Weather

In a season of onions in the months
of winter, we brought a bitter broth
to boil with basil leaves and pepper.

Mountains iced with fir
trees pointed through the clouds
and telephone wire sang those heights
insect laments of summer.

We went upon a highway (flurries
dove in the wind) in a dust-
colored car, tires laden with chain,
to a bare patch of strawberry

like blood beneath a wound of snow.

It was the secret of this cold what seeds
would spring up where we stood, prisoners
whose minds held histories
of other climates, other times.

We carried mattocks
on our shoulders, shovels in our hands—
the grave hung closed for us to sever all

the roots of that ground like a tangle of ginger.

We gave her back the earth
in death, a stone to call our kitty's name, icon
to not forget. Where we can never step
again, there is a scattering of sunburnt needles.

Having entered an autumn of ghosts
who gesture into air,
there are many afternoons we sit in wonderment
over dry spells, or sudden torrents,

our tonsils aching in speech
of things we fear to see.
Feeling these absences linger, a scent of pine,
beyond whatever we can bear,

there comes a time like desert water

when it is past remembering
(when the tongue no longer cares to taste even itself).
Seasons of the years pass in no particular order,
then the farmer milks his sheep

and sheers his goats for wool.
He puts cows out to graze on cinders,
sprinkles the land with his store of grain,
and moves himself into an empty barn, crazy,

like a man turned from butchering in the frost.

A woman stands on a beach, brink of solitude,
of water, drink to answer the thirst of her dreams,
and all she sees is salt.

If it should rain, the bride
must question her husband's kinship,
ask why blood is not the brail that ties.

If the words fall from his lips, invisible,
if reason fails—she will know
the world still worships slaughter
but does not honor the ones it has killed.

Like something on a summer day, a birth

of whistling, a crime of intrigue,
we point to each other
without knowing what we mean.

Time stands fallow, around us motions
of weather enter the dirt, and we
collect what mystery we can—
confounded corpse of spirits gone mad in a folly of air.

Easter

If ice turned from itself
to water, touched and turned away,
the air would be forced to carry it on over
where nothing is itself:

> sounds—scraping tree limbs,
> a rustle of green twigs encased by ice skins.

The day he skated beneath the light
skim on the fish-eye lake,
there was a rain of ice in the city streets.
Black umbrellas frosted
in reflections along storefronts
at noon, dusk had fallen,
and the vapor lamps already spewed blue fog.

It was then that a car veered
to the railing, and the mother's head
sank into the husband's lap.
The infant flew through glass,
was cradled on a rough geode:

> the water on the road, the flashlights
> bleaching the red flares black.

It happened as a blade tested
the surface of that lake,
a bird landed on snow in the concrete city:

> it froze at once, so foreign
> was its blood—pure liquid, a clear spring
> with the taste of rain.

Waiting for Granddaddy to die
my eyes cast over objects and try
to discover whatever lives in gifts
of the past, to extract the life that stays
embedded and send it away as mist

to where he lies in place of waking or sleep,
a deep limbo.

When they drag that lake, they will find nothing:

>dressed for cold, a black body
>still tied to skates, entwined in wool,
>a stocking cap over a face.

When they drag that lake looking for something akin
to the sight of carp warped through ice,
they will find that the body bulges off the bones at death
—that after the winter the dead surge up

>as curio, as artifact of the life of flesh.

Circuit of the Intruder

First Vision
Together in this dream, we are
that clearing to the quick
center which is the darkness
chosen for our journey;
we are that which sheds all light.

When we are safe and our victims
motionless, bright with blood,
I look at you sliced with the battle,
your eyes half-shut, swollen,
and the first color of bruise
surfaces as I think:

if my hands
could smooth our footsteps from the path,
you would let me go.

But no, the blood falls black, precise.
Who are you?
My insides steam as I am opened
to the night. It is my body opened,
my body bleeding, and there is no wound
to tie off. I am wholly alive
with the scent of death.

Turned into darkness, we are that
vision itself
which is the emptiness
of sense; we are that
passage led to nothing,
so narrow, the vein follows the blood.

Second Vision
I am alone. The road is red
and the spit of white snow.
The road, the visible sensed not seen, is gravity

and friction. And as the snow thickens,
I turn into its light.
It is like the vision first seen of this night,
but it is so different.

Third Vision
I have guessed your name.

The bodies of fireflies
you rip apart with your thumbnail,
stick the ghastly flares to my pulse—
how you are driven to touch
my wrists and neck, the tender
dents behind each ear, with such spoils of light.

Fourth Vision
Socket where the tongue tastes salt,
nightmare like a clot;
my legs ache with need to walk.
There is mildew kept beneath fitted sheets,
a tooth traded for copper.
Why are you back?

Neither of us is really asleep. Dreaming,
our eyes shake coins in the pockets
of cripples, bottle caps in tins
of the blind. Beggar,
you have spent too many hours here.
Go and make your bed on a hill
where the moon fattens to disappear.

Firefly

When I was a child
on the Wilderness Road
going fast to where my mother came from,
to the place I was to go,
the winding made me sick.
I learned to lean out windows, by sight
send the car head-on—
that sense as if we went straight paths
not taking the hairpin turns.
Clear, sometimes, up fire cherry bark, up
blasted walls past signs that read,
Watch for Rocks that Fall,
my open eye could shoot a scarlet tanager,
a cat-faced leaf, an arrow through a whitetail's heart.

In the thorned locust and beech thatch
were spots the sun leaked to wash my eyelids
with swatches of color.
Light blinked in the open patches, hard rain
drummed the hood, or I would puzzle
blotches of blue space, the quick
reshapings of cloud.

There were things we passed I wanted to touch:
to tilt a jar outside the car and catch some
mountain fog of a morning, or trap a bobwhite call,
a viceroy, a lucky buckeye.
The first time I flew,
I wanted to take the blue Ball jar.

When I felt bad in the backseat swing,
smelling gas mix with Mother's perfume,

Daddy, too, rolled his window down.
Then he'd forget, not use the vent, and cigarette
ash would sting my face.
I'd see the red specter cool,
look through its flicker
to the woman rocking on her porch
and see the pipe smoke spoken forth.

From this moment, if I turned
my head to the fireflies
spun over the grass before dew,
I'd see the flint of the field split from it
in a spell of breeze, see
a tree's twin tops sway as they were lifted
at the break of eventide.

There, as we'd pass a tent meeting
where the voices had risen at once and died,
I'd be emptied of the wish to wear gold
bellies of fireflies stuck on my hands
and throat, to save their dazzle in jars.
Emptied of looking into darkness
for the little lights that fell farther
behind the car, there'd be nothing
I wanted;
a maple leaf splayed on my palm like a star.

for my parents

The Night-Father Was Found Alive

Of sense and outward things,
Fallings from us, vanishings

—Wordsworth

1.
The child lay freezing in snow
not feeling the cold
or the hollow of ice
she formed lying in darkness
behind the house.
She heard her parents' voices call
the name they'd given
and saw the headlights of their car
pass in the air between her and the stars.

As heat dissolved, her body
sank. She could no longer lift
her arms above her head
to wave them into wings.

2.
The night the father took a kitchen knife
to reason with the mother,
the child sat in a pink chair crowded with ballerinas
and screamed until she could not speak
or hear. The father whispered
he wouldn't hurt her, winked,
letting the blade glint with the little light
he stood to hide in the door.
The mother packed her clothes and cried,
"Hush, I'll take you with me, hush now."
The father said they'd never leave alive,
and they didn't.

That was when she killed him.
The child learned to keep silent, still,
and watch him like a movie screen
from which she could not look away.

3.
But in the field years later, numb,
when the voices stopped calling
her home, and windows in the house she'd left
disappeared one by one,
when the child was left alone—
into the clearness of the night,
she shouted to the little lights so far away
how much she hated her father.
Three times she chanted, in a hoarse whisper first.
The voice filled her throat and ached
for the words to be spoken.

A flashlight found her
staring toward blank sky—
the father finding her at last
in the last place he thought to look
before he closed his eyes.
He took the child up on his back, carried her
and sat before a fire,
rubbing her blue feet between his hands
until she could feel his touch again.

Some Day When It Is Dark

This Dreaming, this Somnambulism
is what we on Earth call Life . . .
   —Thomas Carlyle

We wake, and it has come to pass:
the morning dark as glass,
the stars, a two-dimensional paradigm,
the moon, our obscure aviatrix, has left—
her trails lead us to the ocean floor,
the sun, a conundrum of light, is at rest.

It has come to claim us:
the reversal of sight,
the northern way of winter—arctic circle
fanned in rings has rayed
until the south is eaten, flayed.

It is what you told me would happen
but not the same—the prophecy
is answered but feared
like the first name of God;
it has brought forth power obtained
by knowledge. It is no accident;
this is explained magic, a logic.
Can it work again?

Someday when it is dark, you say,
there's something left unsaid.
And it begins to rain. The light goes
farther aloft, flickers, and clouds
come close to ground. We listen.
We take that blue jar I kept for this
and scoop up cloud
like so many sparks. We punch
no holes, we let it go only because
we cannot see how it changes shape—
the glass strained between us.

I think I see in darkness
by instinct, by touch.
I go blind by degrees. Is it your fault,
your will? You will not
offer both hands for touch.
This is the past, a mask of desire,
a mask. This is the past.

Now, the future hangs absolute, dead,
the valley hung with the absence of day,
filled in, opaque mist.
Our houses sit edging the valley ridge.
When we wake in darkness, we remember
all we have said
and sleep the future past,
sleep, the chosen path.
And the present slips
like light stained through glass
or the elemental falling dream caught fast,
caught fast in time itself
at last, at last, at last.
And we are undone, not measured or asked
but passed as flesh
right through the fire,
as fire through glass is passed as fire.

Mothlight (1963)

Brakhage, the crackle of Matisse
unexpected at a museum's
turn. Exposition, explosive
coloring, unclouding the vision.
Sphere light:
mote taken from the eye's
insight; bone seeing;
to see what the sun saw,
insists itself to be.
Animal lumen, the insect's certain
rhythm; flight dust, its attempt
at adherence to any thing other
than itself, to some thing
clearer, defined, sheer.
First lesson:
a collection of luna moths,
corsages pinned to night.
In a fluster of swatches,
in micro-flashes seen once
from the backseat of a car
as it raced against sunlight—
when colors flailed the lids,
rice thin, like antelope prayers—
aboriginal trances, entrapments
of praise:
this dying lilt, sere death
at the hands of light; disintegration's
luminosity—*moth light*—nothing more;
this nature lore, this shadow
study to purify:
dissection of ear-shattering decibel
beam, splitting itself by
frame, by flame.

A Wilderness of Light

Remember the moth, a spot of fire
tossed live in the light last night
above the stage, after the crowd
had gone—up there, flung
into one of the heat lamps: tangible lumen.
Its body lost the dust of wings,
dusting down like sunlight sometimes will
core open a spout in clouds, illumine
a single ailanthus on a hill.

Remember ibises on the edge
of a saltwater marsh, hung
in the willow among Spanish moss,
part of the tree,
like prayers that sing so without sound,
distantly, aroused to flee—
no one sees what causes them to leave.
Sound does not carry here, like a shot
in the dark rings: ibises, white
dinosaurs, this vision: remember the glossed tree,
its camouflage of wings, its disappearance
while it held still spirits an instant
before the breeze rushed the leaves
and a hundred ibises fled as one,
left the tree alone.

Remember the prayer of the spirit,
that promised intercession of tongues
for which we must remember to ask: prayer
that enters our weariness, our mouths
as breath and leaves, having found us out,
to announce the wordless, articulate
spirit, the body's lone act of thanks.

Phenomena, a Photograph

White mountains of feather, live,
white ashes, curled furs—the birds withdrawn
to islands: each alone,
a separate whooper swan.
But this field, snow filled, iced
and fringed with detail
is the island humming: Hokkaido.

There have been things similar:
the crusty bales of hay rowed
into the distance, but they were not
white like this but earth
and dry green. They were not living,
though once they were thought
to have been fjäll asleep
under army blankets.

And leaves have fallen red; red
splat on the wet sidewalk when that
brightness would have changed to brown,
but lingered instead there
on the walk. Step. Steps are
over the color like the rain
that cannot miss—the rain that fades
away the warmth
of fall and brings frost to it, to us.

There are other things; the connections,
the principles unexplained go on,
and have they been seen
or are they to be seen—we hope and linger
like the red leaves in the rain:
the silent, mushroom dream
rising like a rain cloud, seeded
like the furrowed field in spring.

Late summer, some walked into the corn
and felt the day crumble underfoot.
Among dry stalks and mud hills
was the scene of some scourge
just come or gone, some plague
having gutted the husks. But we knew it was
not the presence of anything different
that had it done—the dried corn rotted inside—
but the absence of water. How the
scorched foliage speared legs,
and the hollow shafts would not bear our weights
or conceal us in the far field,
flung into the farmers' fields, trespassing
as we would have them trespass
only to walk a longer way home
past the barren sight of corn, the snap
of each branch broken by our grasps on the ground,
past the absence of color without being white—
straw—taller than our arms upraised—shrouds
and echo of abandoned harvest.

We were then the lichen on the land,
but the plants had been so long deadened,
except when the wind rattled,
we waited then for cattails
instead
for milkweed pods to burst dry breaths
like dust like frost like anything
so mysterious, so delicate
here and there, open and away,
airborne, a soft and lingering kiss disclosed.

And when the pods had burst a week ›
we left the fjeld for the mountain ridge.
And in the brown fall, the yellow
end of fall, we noticed the places of fir,
the warm green, the new needles, their
soft insistence—come touch—come touch—

in the midst of decay and the crisp
dusty forest, our feet shuffle made speak.

That green invitation is the closest
we have met with that message which is blessed.

Let snow blow on, an element with frail
character, icy figures to impel
with the wind
with the wind.
Let snow, like sound, drift and mound
and rise and fall where birds are and are not all.
Let the field be moved and ruffed
and ridged as if it were a sea
covered in midstorm, stilled.
And perhaps this is a sea, or will
be one with thaw,
when the photograph whispers its name:
What I was before this instant, so I am now,
and the instant after this is all I was, is all.
The slight movement sensed,
or the busy interruption of all motion
that occurs again and again,
itself phenomena, a photograph.

So the sea becomes a sea
and the whooper swans speak,
their tiny eyes roll
and wave, wings start up like trees
in the shadow of trees
and several craned, looped heads
breeze into the morning like an evaporation
of snow water
rising in the steam of a shared dream.

These swans go somewhere south, drift down
like feathers trilled through rain
like their orange beaks burrowed

into their own breasts again
like their voices sing   cry   speak in the silence
of the rain.

And let the snow drift
and the new sea be raised
in the pure image, let exposure take place
of nothing, the record
of whiteness itself only white—
the witness in everything, in each
the light come true again and again—

Let the new sea be raised.
Let praise begin: let it rain, let it rain.

Water Burning Wills Away

Sunset blazes the mountains, an ice of fire
edges each petal of land as it peels back the distance
shaped of these hills. If we walk down to the bridge
built on a sink hole but holding still, if we chance
to meet for the relief there of talking ourselves into dusk,
the creek, crisp as leaves, a chink beneath us,
will be burnished by the sure-burning sky. This day
will quicken with the lengthening of light, cold snap.
Our faces scrubbed with chill luffa will flush; the quail
vault as a breeze laps the surface of the half-frozen creek,
and our eyes tense on specks of flight. Geese float by,
speckled fish, this essence of talk: it might look to us
like a spreading of blood, the red-lit serpent swirling past
and away; it might look like the end of the days, terribly
swift; it might just thrash under the bridge where we watch
the century turn white in riffs, almost blue, electric.
What we say sounds close to silt. Silence, no matter,
taps out the depths, smooth stones rock clean by cool, cool
touch, and jagged shale skips the best. At the edge
of winter, tilted toward water, clarity sharpens, arches
like a comet, and we know what we mean. One thing is certain,
as we pick through our reflections, pass our hands in the silk
tail of a comet or the rose tint of snow, like ash
we sift, once spun off the icy sphere as it hurled
cross the night—earth rivets the flailing scarf
blown by the sun's strokes of wind—earth splits the trail
at the ecliptic; there is no gaseous scratch
of death; in 1812, literate inhabitants cheer,
click glasses of comet spirit. Here, here, if we may
will away the ache of the days like water under the bridge,
if we may enter this stream, this new year, lift glasses
of wine, water will heal the wound of the palm,
may mark the dirt banks but wander on and on by no force
save the absence of inertia—even gravity can be charmed.

So saved, also, are we by this balm of motion,
this conversation, this circle of friends
gathered in the flame and babble, by water.

for Tom and Mary Ellen Atkins

Raking with Leaves in the Wind

Raking with leaves in the wind,
it does not matter where our bodies have been.
Skin, old bones and sinew—
there it is beside me in a ship,
and it whispers: remember, remember
you are whipping up leaves with a rusty rake
and the fork slides off and the stick flies
away with the prism of leaves, in the wild, west wind.
And there it is, the whisper: it does not matter
where our bodies have been, where you are now
have you been, have you been
as simple as spring, as the green leaf fell?
I once was a whore,
now I till red soil: remember, on a ship in winds,
the shape of the air is belied in sails,
where we have been, we have been
in our minds,
when our bodies fall away in the end, in the end.
But the sailing?
It is an exercise, my friend.
But the flairing through space?
An elaborate singe.
But the touch of skin?
It is nothing
to the way you will mingle in the end, in the end.
But the body we grieve, and the recognized face?
Prism you cherish, luxury of wind—
a proof of grace, it is
remembrance of distinctions,
a sign that each individual whit
will find its way hence.

Past Visions, Future Events

Come back, angels. Inhabit those trees
where you were so still, not any leaf
other than at rest. I have passed the test
of remembrance, when the vision of trees
as angels, or angels as trees, hidden in branches,
has haunted me beyond the suspect. I am not at rest,
everything I touch is motion. Heart of nerves,
eyes that smart to see what once they beheld
so easily, and the tongue of visions itself lies
listening to speech not just, when once
it spoke of mysterious events that uttered
forth belief, that incurred flame.
Come back, angels. Inhabit those trees
where you sat so silent, where you hoodwinked
me, captive. I was afraid,
afraid of what you made me know was true,
beyond belief. Sometimes, when I find no sleep,
your presence lingers, but it is outside
glass, shadows against the panes.
I cannot let you enter, and you will not
pass. I must watch the shadows
lengthen of your wings' ascent, just without
my field of vision. Peripherally, you shift
in memory, and when I look to recollect,
exactly, your message, it has changed, or I have
charged and cannot be sure I was not in a dream
when I came upon those wondrous stalks
on a slight hill, in the spring air of fall.
A grove of thirty trees where no trees
stood, an assembly of angels
as ordinary branches, trunks tall and sequined
leaves. Leaf and branch, snarled root
and morning squirrel. A flicker knocking,
knocking against a tree. You called

to me to listen and I was filled with prayer.
May I repeat your message, may I
repeat that sting of air—
prayer of kindling, signal of sentient
singing. *Don't leave,* you said, *this grove, fulfilled,*
is your wish for fruit. Live here, stay,
be sure of us, we are real, as real, we are
here when the whole world is at bay.
There's rest just now, and then
a time will happen
when you will be brought to bear—.
Be still, said the trees, *and listen well.*
There will happen to you a call of clear rhythm,
a beckoning. And until it does,
farewell, farewell:
Climb up into the branches and build your nest,
look up to the mountain from whence cometh
your help. But I am frail as fern,
and I will fail if you leave me here.
We're going now.
A forest of angels ascending leaves the trees
as shaken as children left to schooling.
Past visions, I turn to future scenes
remembering the vision, turning
the event of a single day into a steady dream.
But I am frail as fern, and still I say,
inevitably, come back, angels. Inhabit those trees
where you knocked me silly for a second,
out of breath, where you stamped your seal,
invisible incuse, so I would forever
tune one ear, trust one eye to the motion
out of time—be the storm, a brewing willow,
a blade in space to the whim of scrip.

Volume 13: Jirasek to Lighthouses

We are not realists. We are not idealists.
We are intermediatists—that nothing is real,
but that nothing is unreal: that all phenomena
are approximations one way or the other
between realness and unrealness.

—Charles Fort, *The Book of The Damned*

Jirasek, Alois (1851–1930), Bohemian, novelist.
Temno (*Darkness*), his best; 1915.
Jirgalanta (Dzhirgalantu), Jirja (Girga), Jitterbug,
Jiu (Jiul)—from Mongolia through Egypt
to jive to Romania, the river, Jiu, a tributary
of the Danube through the Transylvanian Alps.
Travel the gorge through the Vulcan pass.
The land is old, the railroad winds
shepherds' schists, the ragged granites ground
to a road. The railroad follows the old river route,
the cut of centuries. We have found our way
by barter, by way of a sharp bend in the Nile,
by swing and snycopated 4/4 time. The way is rough
from Jirasek to Lighthouses, it's a shot in the dark.
Our stops are short, abrupt. By morning, we will blink
by the sea.

A spare light beckons, we move, we want to be
the sheltered flame, center
of five-dimensional darkness. The up and down ways,
the strict divide of sky and water, that curving line
into time, arch of a diver, circling time, space-
time, in space, in time. Our minds
moving through the night. Sailing, and the crude lure
jutting vertical, a cone on the flatness of sand.
Our range of light, found.

No one can live here. We think we must whisper.

Where. There's a place
we are traveling where we are traveling
there and there is no place like that place
on earth. Do you know that where? That here, there?
That real sand on real land, and there is water
promised, isn't there land? Oh yes, and fragrant bananas
and water buffaloes, variegated calypso
with purple, pink, yellow. Moonfish, -flowers, and
showers of periwinkles foretold. Hog-heaven.

City of throat slashers, hang onto your hats.
We are moving across the darkness at the constant
rate of one parsec per second (3.26 light years
per 1/60th minute). Unrealness. That is, between realness
and unrealness is the infinite intermediate, the solid
imaginary line divided by Chinese brush strokes.

We'll never get *there*, but no matter what.
The way is rough from Jirasek to Lighthouses,
it's a shot in the dark.
It's probably illusory.

That Idea of Visiting Places in Dreams

*"It was something more than that . . . all the real
part of your life has a real dream in it;
some of the real dream part of you coming true."*

—Dorothy M. Richardson, *The Tunnel*

I said, "I dreamed the strangest dream."
You heard, "I dreamed I married a stream."

My spoken dream I could not tell, the dream
I would have told I dreamed (not the real
dream), the dream you heard I had, the dream
you would have heard me tell (not the real
dream), and that dream we know so well:
the dream between the dreaming edge,
the one real dream we mean to share.

I choose the dream you heard,
to have dreamed, that idea of a stream.
Because love is strictly a travelling.
As Lawrence would have it, so I dare:
it is a dream about marriage.

I will speak it out of the substances
of earth, if the glitter
of fireflies in night leaves
is such. As we near the bridge
I hear water saying its name over
the roots of trees, the rocks
of its passage, and I speed my walk
to its message no matter
what it sings, but I cannot stop
in the dark, muggy breeze to reason
these secrets beneath the bridge because
my head is up and up is all
in this dark, away at the bend
of water, above its circling,

I send my thoughts—there
are the stars of a current
of fireflies humming the damp, night green.
Whittling the foliage, first seen
and then unseen, they matter
more to me in this part
of my dream: I know you,
you are coming after and will see
for yourself this watery dark
of earth and the lights of insects.

At this thought, I stop
for you to catch up. The wait is short,
there is little talk, I take your hand,
you give it back. "Today," I tell you,
"coming up the drive
I heard a bobwhite call and call."
You answer, "So did I."

for Richard